PHILIP'S *Red Books showin...*

LOCAL STREET ATLAS

ASHFORD TENTERDEN

APPLEDORE · BETHERSDEN · BRABOURNE LEES
CHALLOCK · CHARING · HAMSTREET · WOODCHURCH · WYE

CONTENTS

www.philips-maps.co.uk

First published in 2004 by
Estate Publications

This edition published by Philip's,
a division of Octopus Publishing Group Ltd
www.octopusbooks.co.uk
2–4 Heron Quays, London E14 4JP
An Hachette Livre UK Company

Second impression 2008
15/11-04

ISBN 978-0-540-09358-8

© Philip's 2008

Ordnance Survey®

This product includes mapping data licensed
from Ordnance Survey®, with the permission
of the Controller of Her Majesty's Stationery
Office.© Crown copyright 2004. All rights
reserved. Licence number 100011710

No part of this publication may be
reproduced, stored in a retrieval system or
transmitted in any form or by any means,
electronic, mechanical, photocopying,
recording or otherwise, without the
permission of the Publishers and the
copyright owner.

To the best of the Publishers' knowledge, the
information in this atlas was correct at the
time of going to press. No responsibility
can be accepted for any errors or their
consequences.

The representation in this atlas of a road,
track or path is no evidence of the existence
of a right of way.

Ordnance Survey and the OS symbol are
registered trademarks of Ordnance Survey,
the national mapping agency of Great Britain

Printed in China by Toppan

C000128732

Symbol	Description
	...te
	...oad
	Minor Road
	Pedestrianized / Restricted Access
	Track
	Built Up Area
	Footpath
	Stream
	River
Lock	Canal
	Railway / Station
●	Post Office
P P+	Car Park / Park & Ride
C	Public Convenience
+	Place of Worship
→	One-way Street
i	Tourist Information Centre
8 8	Adjoining Pages
	Area Depicting Enlarged Centre
	Emergency Services
	Industrial Buildings
	Leisure Buildings
	Education Buildings
	Hotels etc.
	Retail Buildings
	General Buildings
	Woodland
	Orchard
	Recreational / Parkland
	Cemetery

Boughton Street
Dunkirk
Rough Common
Wickhambreaux
Elmsted
S GATE
Harbledown
Canterbury
Ickham
Wingham
Staple
Ash Marsh
Selling
Chartham Hatch
Thanington
Littlebourne
A257
W
Old Wives Lees
A28
Bekesbourne
Shottenden
Chartham
Nackington
Patrixbourne
Bridge
Goodnestone
Know
Chilham
Shalmsford Street
Adisham
Chillenden
Nonington
A252
Bishopsbourne
Aylesham
Tilma
Molash
Petham
B2068
Lower Hardres
Kingston
Womenswold
Elving
Godmersham
Upper Hardres Court
Barfreston
Bilting
Sole Street
Bossingham
Barham
Woolage Green
Eyt
Boughton Aluph
Cruddale
Waltham
Derringstone
Shepherdswell or Sibertswold
A28
Hassell Street
Stelling Minnis
Denton
Coldred
A2
Wh
7
Wye
Bodsham
Wootton
Lydden
A2
ennington
Elmsted
Rhodes Minnis
Elham
Ewell Minnis
Temple Ewell
Hastingleigh
Lymbridge Green
Swingfield Minnis
Alkham
Buck
Brook
Stowting
West Hougham
10
Hinxhill 11
Brabourne
Densole
B2
llesborough
South llesborough
10
Brabourne Lees
Lyminge
Paddlesworth
Hawkinge
Capel-le-Ferne
A20
4
15
Postling
Etchinghill
Channel Tunnel Terminal
13
East Wear Bay
Mersham
Sellindge
1·7
Stanford
11
Newington
11
A2
12
Cheriton
Aldington Frith
E. Stour River
B2068
A20
M20
Folkestone
Aldington
Saltwood
Sandgate
Bonnington
Lympne
Saltwood
Bilsington
B2067
Lympne
A261
S HYTHE
Hythe
Ruckinge
Hythe
Burmarsh
Newchurch
Romney Marsh
A259
Dymchurch
St Mary in the Marsh
Ivychurch
St Marys Bay
New Romney
Old Romney
B2075
Littlestone-on-Sea
Greatstone-on-Sea

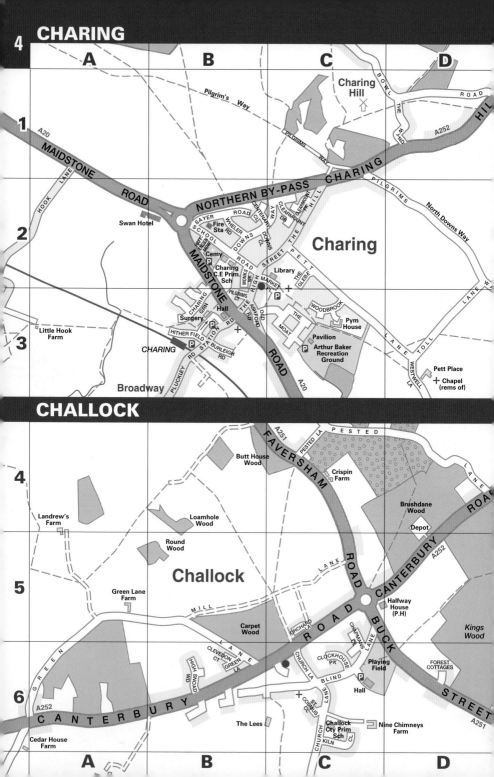

CHARING

A   B   C   D

Pilgrim's Way

Charing Hill

BOWL ROAD

THE WIND

PILGRIMS WAY

A20

MAIDSTONE ROAD

A252

CHARING HILL ROAD

NORTHERN BY-PASS

CHARING HILL

PILGRIMS WAY

North Downs Way

HOOK LANE

Swan Hotel

SAYER ROAD

WHELER RD

CENTENARY CL

CLEARMONT CL

AVE

THE DOWNS CL

CLEARMONT DR

HIGH STREET

THE PETT

Charing

Fire Sta

SCHOOL ROAD

ASHER CMSS

Cemy

Charing C.E Prim. Sch

MONKS WAY

HIGH STREET

MARKET

Library

THE GLEBE

TOLL LANE

WESTWELL LANE

CHARING GRN

Hall

PILGRIMS CT

THE ASHFORD RD

WOODBROOK

Surgery

HITHER FIELD RD

STATION RD

BURLEIGH RD

THE MOAT

Pym House

Pavilion

Arthur Baker Recreation Ground

Pett Place

Chapel (rems of)

CHARING

PLUCKLEY RD

Broadway

MAIDSTONE ROAD

A20

Little Hook Farm

CHALLOCK

A   B   C   D

A251

FAVERSHAM ROAD

PESTED LA

PESTED LANE

LANE

Butt House Wood

Crispin Farm

Brushdane Wood

ROAD

Landrew's Farm

Loamhole Wood

Round Wood

Depot

A252

CANTERBURY ROAD

Challock

LANE

BUCK ROAD

Halfway House (P.H)

Kings Wood

Green Lane Farm

MILL LANE

Carpet Wood

ORCHARD LANE

CHAPMANS LANE

CLOCKHOUSE PK

Playing Field

FOREST COTTAGES

GREEN LANE

CLEVEDON CT

GREEN LA

HIGH SNOAD WD

BLIND LANE

CHURCH LA

Hall

STREET

A251

A252

CANTERBURY

The Lees

Challock Cty Prim Sch

CHURCH LANE

COSMUS CL

KILN

Nine Chimneys Farm

Cedar House Farm

A   B   C   D

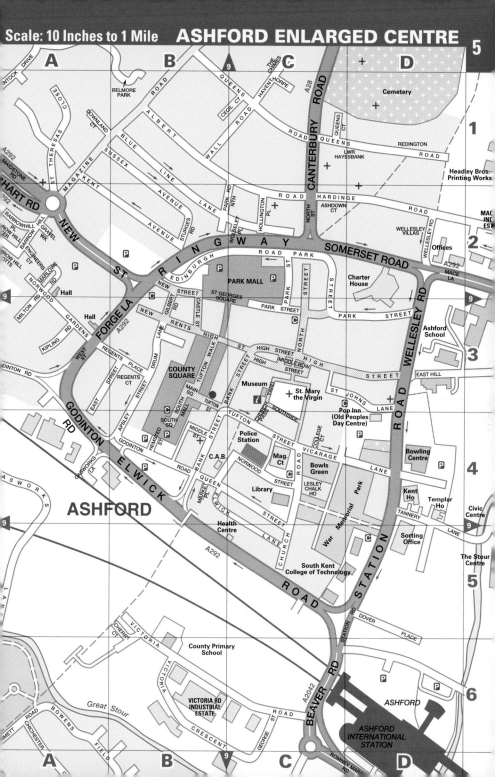

Scale: 10 Inches to 1 Mile   ASHFORD ENLARGED CENTRE

A **B** **C** **D**

1
2
3
4
5
6

Westwell Court

Sewage Works

Nash Court Cottages

Shottenden Farm

Water Works

Castle Farm

Crouchers Manor

Sandyhurst Farm

Club House

Potters Corner

Hoads Wood

Eyesend Plantation

Dogkennel Plantation

Aviary Wood

St Marys (rems of)

Eastwell Lake

Rectory Wood

Eastwell Court

Podberry Wood

Tile Lodge Wood

Pit (disused)

Sand Pit

Playing Field

Lenacre Hall Farm

LENACRE LANE

STREET

LENACRE

KINGSLAND LANE

LANE

SANDYHURST

Eureka Science & Business Park

NICHOLAS RD

TRINITY ROAD

HURST

Bockhanger

Offices

Grosvenor Hall

Police Training College

MAIDSTONE RD

M20

WESTWELL LANE

SANDYHURST LANE

POTTERS

HOADS WOOD GDNS

Ashford Golf Course

GALLOWAY DRIVE

MUSCOVY RD

SISKIN CL

DUNNOCK

SNIPE CL

AYLESBURY

ANGUS DR

GUERNSEY WY

ALDERNEY WY

HEREFORD RD

HAMPSHIRE

PORTLAND WY

BLOOMSBURY CL

DALE CL

HERBRO

P

E   F   G   H

Eastwell Park
Hotel

The
Flying Horse
Inn

WYE   ROAD

A251

PILGRIMS   WAY

ROAD

W Y E

Boughton &
Eastwell C.C.

**Boughton
Lees**

1

Rook Toll

Tower Farm

ROAD

A28

Kempe's
Corner

Rectory
Plantation

Nursery

HARVILLE

RD

2

*Dukes
Spring*

ROAD

Lake
Wood

Park Barn
Farm

3

F A V E R S H A M

Wilmington
Farm

**Goat
Lees**

Ulley Farm

Kennington
Hall

4

HEATHEY LA

TRINITY RD

WAY

JERSEY
CL

SHERWOOD
CL

F A V E R S H A M

GOATLESS RD

The Towers
School

ROAD

GOTELEY MERE VIEW

Playing
Field

LANE

BALL

MILL   LANE

The
Golden Ball

BROADHURST DR

Cricket
Ground Downs View
Cty Inf Sch

OXIER FLD

KINGS
MEADOW

Sports Ground

P

TILE KILN CL

BROOK

GROSVENOR

**Kennington
Lees**

ULLEY   ROAD

ROOKER
CL

UPR VICARAGE
RD

BALL   LANE

CHURCH   RD

ST MARYS
GRV

FIELDS

Graveyard

EAST MOUNTAIN LA

CANTERBURY

5

LOWER
VICARAGE

GLEBE   WAY

FAVERSHAM

Kennington
C.E. Junior
School

ROAD

TRITTON

MARLBOROUGH
WAY

OKEHAMP-
TON CL

TRITTON
CL

TON CL

ORCHARD   LANE

GRASMERE HILL

THIRLMERE

MEADOW BROOK

BROOK

SCHOOL   RD

CHURCH   ROAD

Playing
Field

THE

TRITTON

BIRLING
TONGUES

STREET

HILLCREST
CL

Croft Hotel

6

CROFTON
CL

BRACKEN
CL

PARK VALE

THE
WILLOWS

ASHBORNE
RD

MID
SUMMER
HILL

Kennington

RIDGE

CANON WOOD
WAY

Pilgrims Rest
Hotel

ROAD

BY BROOK

UNDER
WOOD

BELMONT
RD

BURTON
ROAD

GREENBANK

GARDEN
PL

FIELD

WARWICK
RD

NORTH
FIELDS

Spearpoint
Corner

Liby

By

E k
County Schs

TUDOR   ROAD

TUDOR
END

THE

SHEPWAY

WICK RD

ROAD   WAY

10

olmlea
Farm

E   F   G   H

A **B** Marble Wood **C** Eyesend Plantation **D**

The undel

Greensand Way

WATERFALL ROAD

Pigsbrook Wood

GODINTON

Godinton Plantation

A20

HAZEL HEIGHTS

Eyesend

BLOSSOM

HILL RISE

FOREST

LODGE

WOOD

SUN RISE

WYND

AV

1

Balls Wood

Lodge Wood

FOREST

ROSEWOOD

ELMHURST CL

West Lodge

Chestnut Tell Plantation

SPINDLEWOOD

SYCAMORE LA

HEATH WOOD

2

Swinford Manor School

Godinton House

Godinton Park

Jubilee Plantation

Greensand Way

WHITEBEAM CL

MYRTLE GRN

SWEETBAY

HOLLY

ASPEN DR

MDWS

CRESCENT

EVERGREEN WY

River Spinney

BUTTERNUT COPSE

MULBERRY

MAGIC

Godinton Cty Prim. Sch.

LOUDON

ROAD

P Hall

LOUDON WAY

CEDAR

EAST LODGE

LIME

3

Stour Valley Walk

SPRINGWOOD

THE GORSE

LOOKHOLT

SPRINGWOOD

DRIVE

ASH LA

CHESTNUT CL

Willow Bed

AVENUE

THE SPINES

CYPRESS

MAPLE

DRIVE

YEW

HAWREA

Great Stour

Godinton Park

JUNIPER

ROWAN

VIBURNUM CL

BRUNSWI

CHART ROAD

4

NINN

Ninn Lodge Farm

Household Was Disposal Site

Bucksford Manor

A28

CHART BROOKFIELD

BEAVER LA

LEACON RO

Riversi Sch

CLOCKHOUSE

STOURHOUSE CL

CHART LANE

CHART LANE

Cricket Grnd

GREAT CHART BY-PASS

ROAD

B2229

School

OAK LANDS

5

Great Chart

STREET

THE PADDOCKS

THE SINGLETON

CORONATION DR

MIDDLE ROAD

Playing Field

Buxford Mill Hotel

Singleton Lake

HERON WK

COVERT

HONEYSUCKLE

FIELD

BEECH

MEADOW

HOMESTEAD

LANG DALE

LANE

LANE

Court Lodge

THE

PADWELL

HILL CREST

Rec Grnd

HOPPERS WY

HAYMAKERS

YEOMANS SQ

MILL FLD

LITTLE HEMPEN

BARBERS

OXEN LEASE

ORCHARD

CULTER FELD

HEATH

CLEVES LA

6

Friars School

ASHFORD

ROAD

A28

ASHFORD RD

MARAMION

IMPERIAL WY

STOWELL

KIRK VIEW

GRAVELLY FLD

SINGLETON

BLUE FLD

BRADBRIDGE

THE BULRUSHES

WILLOW

DRAGON

HOXTON

HOXTON CL

SINGLETON CENTRE

P

BARN

MANORFIELD

BUCKSFORD

TITHE

REDMAIN

BARNBERRY

BUTTFIELD

MERIDIAN ROAD

BISHOPS

Chart m Sch

MAY PL

A **B** 12 **C** **D**

ASHFORD RD

E   F   G   H

The Warren

6

Bybrook
County Schs

Liby

Sports
Grnd

EUROGATE
BUSINESS
PARK

EUREKA
LEISURE PARK

THOMSON RD

RUTHERFORD

BRADFIELD RD

TRINITY RD

A251

1

M20
JUNCTION 9

Cinema

Motel

M20

Bybrook

NINE

ACRES

Cemetery

WARREN RETAIL
PARK

Ashford
International Hotel

SIMONE

WEIL

AVENUE

DRIVE

Surgery

ROAD

A28

Post House
Hotel

CANTERBURY

ROAD

A28

2

10

St. Teresas
R.C. Prim. Sch

BARROW
HILL

Highworth
School For Girls

BLACK
TOWN

QUANTOCK

MALVERN

PENNINE

CHEVIOT

DOVEDALE
CT

CHILTERN

QUANTOCK

DRIVE

BELMORE PK

BROOME RD

BASKERVILLE

QUANTOCK
THE
WEALD

ROAD

NORTH
BROOKE

NORTHBROOKE LA

Cemetery

QUEENS

QUEENS

QUEENS
ROAD

Headley Bros.
Printing Works

Sports
Ground

Great Stour

3

HEN
INDU
ES

HIGH

WESTERN AV
DAY HOSPITAL

CHART
RD

TEMPLAR

MAIDSTONE RD

MEADOW RD

QUANTOCK

ROAD

ST THERESAS

MAZINE

ALBERT

BLUE LINE LA

SUSSEX AV

KENT

ROAD

HARDINGE RD

MACE
IND EST

Playing
Field

Fire
Sta

RIVERSIDE
IND EST

MACE   LANE

4

10

H

St Mary's
C.E. Prim
Sch

Rec
Grd

RINGWAY

SOMERSET
RD

Ashford
School

EAST

CANTER
BURY

WALLIS R

HOBBS WOOD
IND EST

UNSWICK

GODINTON RD
IND EST

FORGE LA

Edinburgh Rd

NEW RENTS

St St Georges
PARK ST

PARK ST

HIGH

STREET

Bowling
Centre

Civic
Centre

TUFTON RD

MILL COURT

BIRLING

LINDE

STAR

GOR

BROOKFIELD
IND PK

LEACON

MONTPELIER
BUSINESS
PARK

FAIRWOOD
IND EST

GASWORKS

LANE

ELWICK   ROAD

BANKS ST

TUFTON ST

QUEEN

ELWICK

South Kent
College

St JOHNS

VICARAGE LA

CHURCH
RD

STATION   RD

Sorting
Office

East Stour

The Stour
Centre

Cycle Track

MILLERS

EAST STOUR

5

RD WY

BAILEYS

CHESTFIELD

Playing Field

Victoria Park

BOWENS
ROAD

CHICHESTER CL

HILLYFIELDS

RISING RD

JEMMETT

CHRISTCHURCH

MUSGROVE

Primary
Sch

VICTORIA
RD

VICTORIA RD
IND EST

GEORGE

Great Stour

Cycle Track

DOVER PL

ASHFORD

ASHFORD
INTERNATIONAL
STATION

Sports
Ground

Depo

ASHFORD

Ashford
Sch

6

A2042

OLD RAILWAY
INDUSTRIAL

Ashford
South C.P.
School

Oak Tree
Sch

The
Learning
Centre

South Kent
College

South Ashford

Rec
Grnd

BOND

MEADOW

WILLIAM

FRANCIS

BARN

PLATT

MAXFIELD

TORRINGTON   ROAD

WHITFIELD

DENMARK

SYDNEY

PROVIDENCE

RIVERSDALE

SOUTH STOUR AV

EAST

MEAD
AV

GODFREY WK

BEAVER   ROAD

NEWTOWN

WAINWRIGHT

NEWTOWN

Nursery

IND
EST

McArthur

E   F   G   H

St Simon's
Prim Sch

Beaver

13

E F G H

Naccolt

Sewage
Works

Appleby
Farm

Bourne Dyke

1

BLACKWALL

ROAD

Sillibourne
Farm

BLACKWALL ROAD

Blackwall
Farm

Great Bromley
Farm

2

SPELDERS HILL

Sales
Wood

Moneytree
Farm

Goodcheap
Farm

3

GOODCHEAP LANE

oose
reen

Plumpton
Farm

Flowergarden Wood

Boarfield
Wood

4

Sweetwillow
Wood

Court Lodge
Farm

Hinxhill

Alders

ROAD

HE WILLIAM HARVEY
HOSPITAL

P

Ouseley

South
Oaks

5

HINXHILL

LANE

Breeches
Wood

BOCKHAM

Quarrington Woods

6

STREET

QUARRINGTON

Supermarket

E F 15 G Bockham
Farm Cottage H

Singleton

Great Chart Cty Prim Sch

Hopewell School

Beaver Green Cty Prim Sch

Bridewell Plantation

Playing Field

Colemans Kitchen Wood

Chilmington Green Farm

Great Chilmington

Chilmington Green

Bartlett Farm

Willowbed Farm

Moat

Court Lodge Farm

Little Court Lodge Farm

Stubb's Cross

ASHFORD
A28

A · B · C · D

M20 JUNCTION

...WAY WORKS INDUSTRIAL ESTATE

HUNTER CL · HUNTE... · LEEZE · ...DS ROAD · ...C · SEVINGTON

TWELVE ACRES ROAD · ROAD WORKS

Subway

Health Centre

RALEIGH · NELSON

A2070 · ROAD

AYLESFORD · ALSOTHERTON RD · BENTLEY · COLLARD · EVANS

NEWTOWN GRN · NEWTOWN RED

NEWTOWN ROAD · BEAZLEY CT · BAXEN DALE CT

Aylesford Green

Play Field

EALHAM... · HIGHFIELD

JULIEN · SHEPHERD · CL · COWDREY CL · ...ICOE · DRAKE

TROU... BRIDGE CL · HARDY · CL · JUDITH RD

CL · MAUR...

ROAD · CROWBRIDGE · MEAR

Swan Centre

TURNER CL

CURTIS · ALBION PL

ALBION PL

Boys Hall

BOYS HALL · ASH GRN · MEAD... · ROMIL STREAM · GRN

LUCKHURST · LANE · ...JUHN · JOHNSON · ROAD · WOLLMER RD

CHURCH · FOLEY CL

KINGFISHER CL · NIGHTGALE CL

MALLAPUR...

MALLARDS

Recreation Ground

GLADSTONE · RD · BATH

CROW... · SWALLOW FIELD · ROAD

ROAD · CROWBRIDGE · PAPER... ...K · BRIDGE

MUNSTEREIFEL

ROAD · ST JOHN'S CT · FOSTER · CHURCH RD · ROAD

CHURCH · BARREY

St Marys

Court Lodge

HERBERT ROAD · HAMILTON RD

ROYDS · HEL... ...BERT ROYDS

EAST... ...R · EARLSWORTH · ROAD

CANTERBURY · SURTEES' · THE COURTYARD

ROAD · ASHFORD BUSINESS PARK

MUNSTEREIFEL · CHURCH · ROAD

Sevington

East C.P.

JACOBS OAK · CLOVER CT · PROSPECT

DRIVE · MONUMENT

THE LONG BARROW

THE BOULEVARD

Moat

WILLOW CL · FAIRVIEW · EAST STOUR · KINGS... ...WAY

BANK WAY

South Willesborough

ORBITAL PARK

HALL AV

Travel Inn

Ashford Market

WAY · THE · PARADE

MUNSTEREIFEL · ROAD · BAD

BAD · MUNSTEREIFEL · ROAD

INLAND CLEARANCE DEPOT (Eurotunnel)

HIGHFIELD · ROAD

A2070

OAD

Ashford Business Point

WATERBROOK · AVENUE

Hogben Farm

East Stour

P C

TRUCK STOP (Ashford Freight Services)

Hillcrest Farm

Sevington Bridges

Bilham Farm

Captain's Wood

Cheeseman's Green Farm

Swanton Mill

Cheeseman's Green

Pattison Farm

E   F   G   H

Supermarket

Swatfield
Bridge
Pilgrims
Hospice

SUMMERHILL
PK

HYTHE

M20

A20

KINGSFORD

LANE

HIGHFIELD

LANE

BOCKHAM

LANE

LANE

Bockham
Farm Cottage

QUARRINGTON LANE

Quarrington
Farm

Moat

1

Spring Wood

Bockhanger
Wood

2

Hatch Park

Longthorne
Farm

Mersham-le-
Hatch

3

LANE

Boyes
Farm

STREET

ROAD

A20

M20

4

Conscience
Farm

BLIND

BLIND

CRANBROOKS

Swanton
Court

Jemmett
Farm

The
Forstal

LANE

STREET

CHURCH

Denne

The
Orchids

Planters
Ter

Kings
Fields

Pond Cl

Burgate
Ter

The
Street

Glebelands

Old Rectory
Cl

The
Oaklands

Mersham

ROAD

BOWER

Church
Cl

Manor
House

Cherry Glebe

Orchard
Cl

Cherry Glebe

Cherry Glebe

ROAD

5

Primary
School

East Stour

LONG ROW

FLOOD

E   F   G   H

6

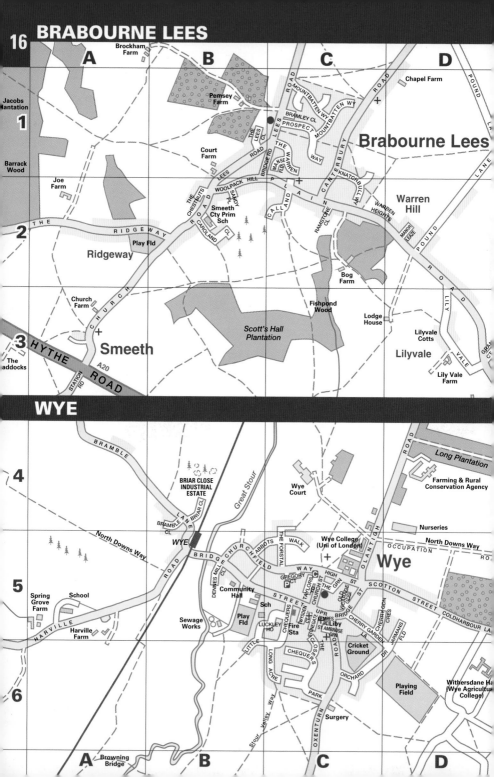

A **B** **C** **D**

Brockham Farm

Jacobs Plantation

1

Barrack Wood

Joe Farm

Pemsey Farm

Court Farm

Chapel Farm

MOUNTBATTEN WY

BRAMLEY CL

THE LEES CL

PROSPECT

MOUNTBATTEN WY

ROAD

CANTERBURY

Brabourne Lees

WAY

WARREN

KNATCHBULL

THE LEES ROAD

BRIDGE RD

MANSE FLD

PLAIN

Warren Hill

WARREN HEIGHTS

MANOR LEAZE

POUND LANE

The Chestnuts

WOOLPACK HILL

SANDY PL

Smeeth Cty Prim Sch

CALLAND

RAMSTONE CL

2

THE RIDGEWAY

ROAD

CAROLAND

CL

Play Fld

Ridgeway

ROAD

Bog Farm

LILY

VALE

GRA CL

Church Farm

CHURCH

ROAD

Fishpond Wood

Lodge House

Lilyvale Cotts

POUND ROAD

3 HYTHE ROAD

STATION RD

A20

Smeeth

Scott's Hall Plantation

Lilyvale

The Paddocks

Lily Vale Farm

BRAMBLE

Long Plantation

ROAD

4

BRIAR CLOSE INDUSTRIAL ESTATE

BRAMBLE LANE

BRIAR CL

Great Stour

Wye Court

Farming & Rural Conservation Agency

Nurseries

North Downs Way

OLANTIGH

North Downs Way

WYE

BRIDGE

ROAD

DENNES MILL CL

CHURCHFIELD

ABBOTS WALK

THE FORSTAL

Wye College (Uni of London)

OCCUPATION RO

Wye

SCOTTON STREET

COLDHARBOUR LA

5

Spring Grove Farm

School

Community Hall

Sch

STREET

CHEQUERS

TAYLORS CL

LYNSTED CL

WAY

GREGORY CT

HIGH ST

THE GRN

CHURCH ST

UPR BRIDGE ST

OLD VICARAGE LA

ST AMBROSE LGRN

SCOTTONS

CHERRY GARDEN

HARMANS FLD

CRES

HARVILLE ROAD

Harville Farm

Sewage Works

Play Fld

LUCKLEY HO

Fire Sta

Cricket Ground

Playing Field

6

LITTLE CHEQUERS

LONG ACRE

CHEQUERS PARK

OXENTURN ROAD

ORCHARD

Surgery

Stour Valley Way

Withersdane Ha (Wye Agricultur College)

Browning Bridge

A **B** **C** **D**

A   **B**   **C**   **D**

Hoddiford Mill

Moorstock Farm

GREENFIELDS

CHISLET LANE

BROOK LANE

1

A20

ASHFORD

THE SADDLERS

Dukes Head

Elmtree Farm

MOORSTOCK LANE

Sports Ground

Potten Farm

Cty. Prim. Sch.

GREEN

SWAN WAY

DOWNS

WHITEHALL WY

LOURDES MANOR

HOMELANDS CL

LEAFIELD CL

FORGE CL

Village Hall

Brook Farm Kennels

2

Rotherwood Farm

Somerfield Barn Court

Richardson Court

SWAN ROAD

● **Sellindge**

Grove Bridge

BARROW HL

MEADOW GR

BARROW HILL RISE

A20

M20

Barrowhill

3

BETHERSDEN

A   **B**   **C**   **D**

Frid Wood

Paris Corner

PLUCKLEY LANE

New Barn Farm

Old Saw Mill

Bateman Corner

Mill Farm

MILL ROAD

ROAD

OLD SURRENDEN MANOR

4

Lamberden Wood

WISSENDEN LANE

Sewage Works

NORTON LANE

Rec Grd

Water Farm

KILN LANE

5

Cty Prim Sch

CHURCH HILL

FORGEFIELD

THE STREET

The George PH

Village Hall

THE FORGE

THE DENE

Lovelace

LOVELACE SCHOOL ROAD

CHESTER AV

BLACK PITS

ORCHARD FIELD

WHISTON AV

Bethersden

ASHFORD ROAD

The Bull PH

Bull Green

Cricket Club

BAILEY FIELDS

Works

ROAD

Hoad's Wood

6

BULL

Low Wood Farm

Island Farm

A28

A28

A   **B**   **C**   **D**

Bridge

Catdref Farm

HARBOURNE LA

Knock Wood

Ingleden

Knock Wood

Coever Farm

Dawbourne Wood

Pope House Farm

POPE HOUSE

A28

ASHFORD ROAD

Primary School

Village Hall

GLEN WOOD CL

HEATHER ROAD

SWAIN ROAD

DRIVE

OX LANE

OX LANE

WAYSIDE AVENUE

JARVIS PL

Rec Grd

MARSHALLS LAND

THE PAVEMENT

GRANGE CRES

GRANGE CRES

ST MICHAELS ROAD

ORCHARD ROAD

SHOREHAM ROAD

LANE

St. Michaels

Silcocks Farm

READERS BRIDGE RD

GRANGE RD

BARNFIELD

AVENUE

LANE

SPRINGFIELD LANE

WEALDEN AV

WEALDEN

OX LANE

SILVER HILL

PARK AVENUE

INGLEDEN ROAD

KNOCKW

HOMEWO

ROAD

WAYSIDE

WAYSIDE

AVENUE

HENLEY WAY

BORESISLE

Fire Station

FIELDS

Playing Fields

CHALK

LESLIE CRES

LESLIE CRES

AVENUE

HENLEY CRES

HENLEY

MEADOWS WAY

STEPHENS

COLONEL

Homewood School

HENLEY

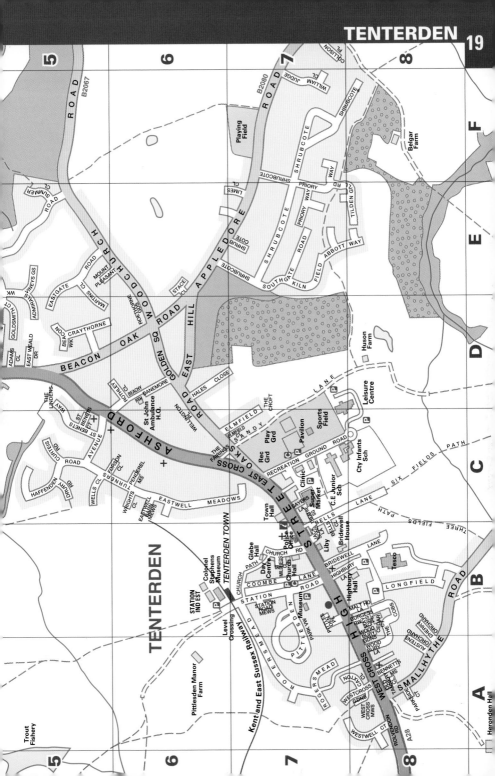

TENTERDEN

Trout Fishery

Heronden Hall

Pittlesden Manor Farm

Kent and East Sussex Railway

TENTERDEN TOWN

Level Crossing

STATION IND EST

Colonel Stephens Museum

STATION

STATION MEWS

CHURCH PATH

COOMBE

ROGERS MEAD

ROGERS MEAD

PARK VIEW MEWS

PITTLESDEN

WESTCROSS

WESTCROSS

WEST CROSS MWS

WESTWELL

POLLENDON RD

A28

WEST CROSS

Church Hall

Day Centre

Glebe Hall

Church RD

WILLIAM

CHURCH LA

MILL

RD

PILLAR BOX

Museum

HIGH

PITTLESDEN

BURGESS

WOOD LA

BURY GDNS

WOOD LA

WOOD LA

BURY LA

BENNETTS

HADLOW

OAK GDNS

GRANT CLS

PARKER

CT

Colic Office

Town Hall

CHURCH

SQ

BRIDEWELL

Bridewell House

Libry

BELLS

BELLS

WEAVERS

Super Market

Clinic

HIGHBURY

LANE

Highbury Hall

BRIDEWELL LA

MALTHO

THE COBS

ASTENS ORCHARD

ORCHARD

CHERRY ORCHARD

Tesco

LONGFIELD

MALLHYTHE ROAD

ST BENETS FT

ST BENETS

ST BENETS

AVENUE

WAY

THE LINDENS

CUTTERS RD

HAFFENDEN RD

DRURY ROAD

WELLS CL

TURNERS CL

PENDEREL CL

WRIGHTS CL

MUSGROVE CL

FORSDEN CL

EASTWELL MEADOWS

EASTWELL MEWS

ASHFORD

ROAD

EAST CROSS

THE FARRINS

Recreation GROUND ROAD

RECREATION

Rec Grd

Play Grd

ELMFIELD

ELMFIELD

THE SANDY

C.E. Junior Sch

Cty Infants Sch

LANE

Pavilion

Sports Field

Leisure Centre

SIX FIELDS PATH

THREE FIELDS PATH

Huson Farm

St John Ambulance H.Q.

WELLINGTON ROAD

HALES CLOSE

THE CROFT

ELMFIELD

DANEMORE PK

BEACHY CL

ROTHLEY CL

GOLDEN SQ

BEACON OAK ROAD

EAST HILL

APPLEDORE

WOODCHURCH ROAD

ROBERTS GS

BEACON WK

CRAYTHORNE

EAST MEALD DR

ADAMS CL

GOLDSMITH CT

ADMIRALS GS

WK

EASTGATE

MOUNT PLEASANT

MARTINS CL

SUMMER WK

ROAD

ROAD

ROAD

B2067

SHRUBCOTE

SOUTHGATE ROAD

KILN FIELD

ABBOTT WAY

PRIORY WAY

PRIORY WAY

WAY

RD

TILDEN GV

SHRUBCOTE

SHRUBCOTE

SHRUBCOTE

LIMES CT

STACE CL

Playing Field

B2080 ROAD

WILLIAM JUDGE WAY

COLLISON PL

Belgar Farm

5 6 7 8

F E D C B A

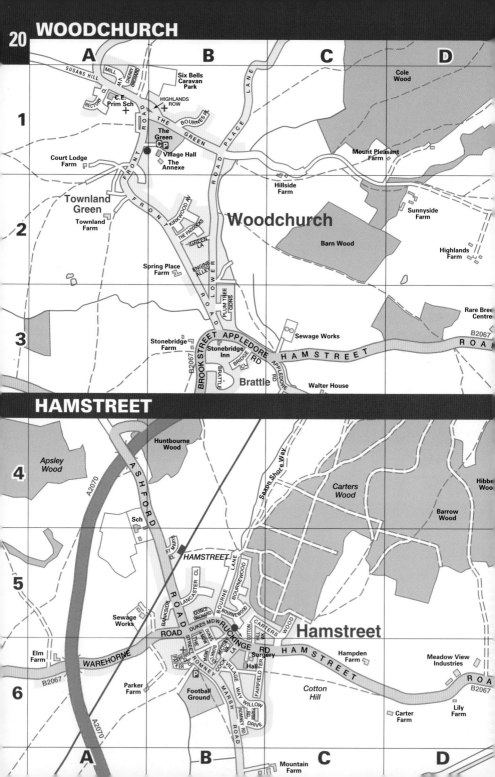

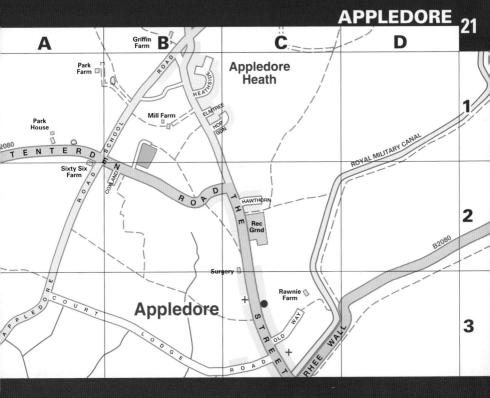

Map labels: A | B | C | D

Griffin Farm

Park Farm

Appledore Heath

Mill Farm

Park House

2080

TENTERDEN

Sixty Six Farm

ROYAL MILITARY CANAL

ELMTREE

HOP GON

HEATHSIDE

ROAD

SCHOOL

COWLAND

ROAD

HAWTHORN

Rec Grnd

B2080

Surgery

Appledore

Rawnie Farm

APPLEDORE COURT

LODGE

THE STREET

OLD WAY

RHEE WALL

ROAD

1 | 2 | 3

INDEX TO STREETS
with Postcodes

22

Richborough Way TN23 12 D3
Richmond Meech Dr TN24 10 A2
Riding Hill TN24 7 E6
Rigden Rd TN23 13 F1
Ringway TN24 5 B2
Ripley Rd TN24 10 C6
Rising Rd TN23 9 F5
River Vw TN23 8 D5
Riverbank Way TN24 13 H3
Riversdale Rd TN23 13 G1
Riverside CI TN23 13 E5
Riverside Ind Est TN24 9 H4
Robert Brundett Dr TN24 10 B1
Roethorne Gdns TN30 19 D6
Rogersmead TN30 19 A7
Roman Way TN23 13 G4
Romney Marsh Rd, Hamstreet TN26 20 B6
Romney Marsh Rd, Park Farm TN23 13 F4
Romney Rd, Hamstreet TN26 20 B6
Romney Rd, Willesborough TN24 10 A5
Romsey CI TN24 10 C4
Romulus Gdns TN23 13 E4
Rookery CI TN24 7 E5
Rosewood Dr TN25 8 D2
Ross CI TN23 13 F2
Rothbrook Dr TN24 6 D5
Rothley CI TN30 19 D6
Rovenden Rd TN30 19 A8
Rowan CI TN23 8 C4
Royds Rd TN24 13 H2
Ruckinge Rd TN26 20 B5
Rugby Gdns TN24 9 H6
Rutherford Rd TN25 9 G1
Rye Ct TN23 12 C1
Rylands Rd TN24 9 H2

Sackville Cres TN23 9 E4
Saddlers Way TN23 13 G4
St Ambrose Grn TN25 16 D5
St Annes Rd TN23 12 D1
St Barnabas CI TN23 13 E1
St Benets Ct TN30 19 C5
St Benets Way TN30 19 C5
St Cosmus CI TN25 4 C6
St Georges Sq TN24 5 B2
St Johns Cres TN24 14 C1
St Johns La TN23 5 C3
St Lukes Ct TN23 13 E1
St Marys CI TN23 20 B5
St Marys Grn TN24 7 F5
St Michaels Ter TN30 18 B2
St Mildreds CI TN30 19 B7
St Stephens Walk TN23 12 D1
St Theresas Clo TN24 5 A1
Sandilands TN24 10 B5
Sandling CI TN23 13 E2
Sandy La, Ashford TN24 10 D4
Sandy La, Tenterden TN30 19 C7
Sandy PI TN25 16 B2
Sandyhurst La TN25 6 A6
Saw Lodge Fld TN23 13 H5
Sayer Rd TN27 4 B2
Sayers La TN30 19 C7
School Rd, Appledore TN26 21 B1
School Rd, Bethersden TN26 17 B6
School Rd, Charing TN27 4 B2
Scotton St TN25 16 C5
Sevington La TN24 10 C6

Shaw Cross TN24 9 H1
Sheepfold La TN23 13 G5
Sheldwich CI TN23 13 E2
Shepherd CI TN23 12 D3
Shepherd Dr TN24 14 C1
Shepway TN24 10 A1
Sherwood CI TN24 7 E4
Shipley Mill CI TN23 13 G4
Shoreham La TN30 18 B1
Shrubcote TN30 19 E7
Silver Birch Grn TN23 13 G4
Silver Hill TN30 10 D4
Silver Hill Gdns TN24 10 C5
Silver Hill Rd TN24 10 C5
Simone Weil Av TN24 9 F2
Simons Av TN23 13 E1
Singleton Hill TN23 8 C6
Singleton Rd TN23 8 B5
Siskin CI TN24 6 D4
Six Fields Path TN30 19 C8
Skylark Way TN23 13 H6
Smallhythe Rd TN30 19 A8
Smithy Dr TN23 13 G4
Snipe CI TN24 6 D4
Snowbell Rd TN23 13 G4
Somerset Rd TN24 5 C2
Sotherton TN24 14 B1
South Bourne TN23 12 D3
South Lea TN23 13 F5
South Mall TN23 5 B4
South Motto TN23 13 G4
South Sq TN23 5 B4
South Stour Av TN23 9 G6
Southgate Rd TN30 19 E7
Southside TN23 5 C3
Spelders Hill TN25 11 H3
Speldhurst CI TN23 12 D3
Spindlewood End TN23 8 C2
Springfield Av TN30 18 D3
Springwood CI TN23 8 D3
Springwood Dr TN23 8 D3
Sprotlands Av TN24 10 B5
Squirrel La TN25 8 D1
Stace CI TN30 19 E6
Stanhope Rd TN23 12 D2
Stanhope Sq TN23 13 E2
Star Rd TN24 10 A4
Station Rd, Ashford TN23 5 D5
Station Rd, Brabourne Lees TN25 16 A3
Station Rd, Charing TN27 4 B3
Station Rd, Tenterden TN30 19 B7
Station Rd Ind Est TN30 19 B6
Station Road Mws TN30 19 B7
Stirling Rd TN24 13 H1
Stonegate TN25 16 C5
Stour CI TN23 8 D5
Stourfields TN24 9 H2
Stowell CI TN23 12 B1
Strouts Rd TN24 12 B1
Studio CI TN24 7 F5
Sturges Rd TN24 5 B2
Suffolk Dr TN23 9 F5
Summer CI TN24 10 B6
Summer Leeze TN24 10 B6
Summer Leeze Gdns TN24 10 B6
Summerhill TN23 12 D2
Summerhill Pk TN24 15 E1
Sun Rise TN25 8 D1
Surtees CI TN24 14 A2
Susans Hill TN26 20 A1
Sussex Av TN24 5 A1

Swain Rd TN30 18 C2
Swallow Fld TN24 14 B1
Swan Grn TN25 17 C2
Swan La TN25 17 C2
Sweetbay Cres TN23 8 C3
Sycamore La TN23 8 C2
Sydney St TN23 9 G6

Tabret CI TN24 7 E6
Tadworth Rd TN24 9 H1
Tally House Rd TN26 12 B6
Tannery La TN23 5 D4
Taylors Yd TN25 16 C5
Taywood CI TN24 10 B5
Templar Way TN23 9 E3
Temple CI TN23 13 E3
Tennyson Rd TN23 13 F2
Tenterden Rd TN26 21 A1
The Boulevard TN24 14 B2
The Bulrushes TN23 8 B6
The Chestnuts TN25 16 B2
The Chimes TN24 5 C1
The Close, Singleton TN23 12 D1
The Close, Wye TN25 16 C5
The Cobs TN30 19 B8
The Copse TN23 8 C3
The Courtyard TN24 14 B2
The Croft TN30 19 D7
The Dene TN26 17 C5
The Fairings TN30 19 C6
The Forstal TN25 16 C5
The Glebe TN27 4 C2
The Green, Woodchurch TN26 20 B1
The Green, Wye TN25 16 C5
The Grove TN24 7 G6
The Haven TN23 12 D3
The High St TN27 4 B3
The Hill TN27 4 C2
The Lees CI TN25 16 B1
The Limes TN23 13 E3
The Lindens TN30 19 D5
The Link TN23 12 B1
The Long Barrow TN24 14 B3
The Moat TN27 4 C3
The Orchids TN25 15 G4
The Paddocks, Ashford TN23 8 B5
The Paddocks, Woodchurch TN26 20 B2
The Parade TN24 14 B3
The Pasture TN24 7 E6
The Pavement TN30 18 C2
The Ridge TN24 7 F6
The Ridgeway TN24 16 A2
The Rise TN23 12 D1
The Saddlers TN25 17 A2
The Spinney TN23 8 D3
The Street, Appledore TN26 21 C2
The Street, Bethersden TN26 17 C5
The Street, Great Chart TN23 8 A6
The Street, Hamstreet TN26 20 B6
The Street, Kennington TN24 7 F5
The Street, Mersham TN25 15 G4
The Street, Willesborough TN24 10 D6
The Warren TN25 16 C1
The Weald TN24 9 G3
The Wickets TN24 14 C1
The Willows TN24 7 E6

The Wynd TN27 4 D1
Theatre Sq TN30 19 C7
Thirlmere TN24 7 E6
Thomson Rd TN25 9 F1
Thornlea TN23 8 D4
Thornton CI TN24 10 C5
Three Fields Path TN30 19 B8
Tilden Gill Rd TN30 19 E8
Tile Kiln Rd TN24 7 E5
Tithe Barn La TN23 8 C6
Toke CI TN23 8 B5
Toll La TN27 4 D3
Torrington Rd TN23 9 G6
Tournay CI TN23 9 E6
Towers Vw TN24 6 D5
Trenchard CI TN24 10 C6
Trinity Rd, Ashford TN25 9 G1
Trinity Rd, Kennington Lees TN25 7 E4
Tritton CI TN24 7 G5
Tritton Flds TN24 7 F5
Troubridge CI TN24 14 D1
Tudor By Way TN24 7 E6
Tudor End TN24 10 A1
Tudor Farm CI TN23 13 F2
Tudor Rd TN24 10 A1
Tufton Rd TN24 9 H4
Tufton St TN23 5 C4
Tufton Walk TN23 5 B3
Turner CI TN24 14 A1
Turners Av TN30 19 C6
Turners Ct TN24 10 B6
Twelve Acres TN24 9 H6
Twysden Ct TN25 16 C5

Ulley Rd TN24 7 E5
Underwood CI TN24 7 E6
Upper Bridge St TN25 16 C5
Upper Denmark Rd TN23 9 G6
Upper Vicarage Rd TN24 7 F5

Vespasian Way TN23 13 E4
Viburnum CI TN23 8 D4
Vicarage La TN23 5 C4
Victoria Cres TN23 5 B6
Victoria Rd TN23 5 B5
Victoria Rd Ind Est TN23 5 B6
Village Way TN30 20 B6
Vincent PI TN24 10 B2
Vineys Gdns TN30 19 E5

Wainwright PI TN24 9 H6
Wall Rd TN24 5 B1
Wallis Rd TN24 10 A4
Walnut CI TN24 7 E5
Waltham CI TN24 10 C4
Warehorne Rd TN26 20 A6
Warren Heights TN25 16 C2
Warren La TN24 9 H4
Warren Retail Pk TN24 9 F2
Warren Vw TN25 9 E2
Warwick Rd TN24 7 F6
Washford Farm Rd TN23 12 D3
Watercress La TN23 8 D6
Watermead CI TN23 13 E1
Waterside TN24 10 C5
Watsons CI TN25 6 D4
Wayside TN30 18 D3
Wayside Av TN30 18 D2
Wealden Av TN30 18 D3
Weavers Way TN30 12 D1
Wellesley Rd TN24 5 D3
Wellesley Villas TN24 5 D2
Wellington PI TN30 19 C6
Wells CI TN30 19 C5

West Cross TN30 19
West Cross Gdns TN30 19
West Cross Mws TN30 19
West St TN23 5 A
Westbourne TN23 12
Western Av TN23 8
Western Gdns TN24 10
Westmoors TN23 12
Westwell Ct TN30 19
Westwell La, Bockhanger TN25 6 A
Westwell La, Charing TN27 4
Wharton Gdns TN24 10
Wheat Ct TN23 12
Wheler Rd TN27 4
Whigham CI TN23 12
Whiston Av TN26 17
White Willow CI TN24 13
Whitebeam CI TN23 8
Whitehall Way TN25 17 C
Whitfield Cotts TN23 9 C
Whitfield Rd TN23 9
Wickenden Cres TN24 10
Willesborough Ct TN24 10 D
Willesborough Ind Pk TN24 10 C
Willesborough Rd TN24 10 A
William Judge CI TN30 19
William Rd TN23 9
Willingdon TN23 12 D
Willow Dr TN26 20 B
Willow Tree CI TN24 10 C
Wilson CI TN24 10 D
Windermere Ct TN24 9 C
Windmill CI TN24 10 B
Wissenden La TN26 17 A
Wivenhoe TN23 12 D
Wolseley PI TN24 5 C
Wood La TN23 13 H
Woodbrook TN24 7
Woodbury Gdns TN30 19 E
Woodbury La TN30 19 A
Woodchurch Rd TN30 19 C
Woodlands Rd TN24 10 B
Woodlea TN24 9 H
Woodside TN23 12 C
Woodstock Way TN24 7 E
Woolmer Dr TN24 14 C
Woolpack Hill TN25 16 B
Woolreeds Rd TN23 13 E
Wotton Rd TN23 13 H
Wrights CI TN30 19 C
Wye Rd TN25 7 H
Wyndham Way TN25 8 B
Wyndy La TN25 8 D
Wyvern Way TN24 10 A

Yeoman Gdns TN24 10 C
Yeomans Sq TN23 8 C
Yew CI TN23 8 B
York Rd TN24 10 A